GW00640729

VEGAN CAKES

VEGAN CAKES   11-25

LIZZY DRIP   SIGN.   21.65

LITTLE GREY DONKEY   SIG. —
  ''   SEA HORSE   '' —
BEACHCOMBERS   '' —

LAVENDER   9.50

JUMBO. AFLOAT   4.50

SHADY DEAL   6.65

BROWN WATER	26.68
GIANT BIRTH + DEATH	12.50
VIRGIN WEEDERS	15.00
AIR EXHUS - EACH	3.50
BRITISH RATTLE SK.1.	95p
PIMP MY RICE	16.50
R.A.F. I-CAM. 1903-1939	7-50